THE COLLEGE
ON THE HILL

THE COLLEGE ON THE HILL

CELEBRATING THE 175TH ANNIVERSARY
OF AMHERST COLLEGE

1821–1996

THE AMHERST COLLEGE ARCHIVES

with an

INTRODUCTION BY

CHARLES C. ELDREDGE '66

AMHERST COLLEGE PRESS   AMHERST, MASSACHUSETTS 1996

This book is dedicated to the memory of Edward
"Doc" Hitchcock 1849, who laid the groundwork
for the College Archives, and to the many alumni
who continue to preserve the history of Amherst.

Cover: College Hill from the Northwest, c. 1878;
J. L. Lovell, Photographers; albumen print,
5¼ x 7⅝ in.

Printed by Thames Printing Co. Inc.,
Norwich, Connecticut

Library of Congress Cataloging-in-Publication Data

The college on the hill: celebrating the 175th anniversary
     of Amherst College, 1821-1996
         p. cm.
     ISBN 0-943184-05-3
     1. Amherst College—Pictorial works. I. Amherst College.
Archives.
LD154.5.C65 1996
378.744'23—dc20   96–9708

To discover the origins of our College Archives, we need only look back to the faculty minutes of September 11, 1851. With a simple motion and vote, Professors Charles Adams and George Jewett were appointed to a committee of two—oh, for such economy today—charged with collecting and preserving all documents pertaining to the history of Amherst College. Their foresight, 145 years ago, has provided us with a wealth of resources, from which we have compiled this delightful collection.

This publication does not pretend to offer scholarship, or a historical narrative, or even a photographic record. It is, in all honesty, a bit of sentiment, of reflection, of short story-telling. I hope you enjoy every page.

The College is indebted to those whose hard work and dedication made this volume possible. Thanks to them, Amherst now has its own keepsake album, a scrapbook like those assembled by its graduates before the advent of the modern yearbook.

It is always possible to question what is here and what is not. But I am confident that those who know and love the College will recognize in this collection the passion for inquiry and discovery, the spark of intellect, and the devotion to a common enterprise that have earned Amherst its truest distinction.

Tom Gerety
President
Amherst College

No photographer awaited the renegade band that arrived in Amherst from Williamstown in 1821, for Etienne Daguerre's invention was still in the future. However, shortly after its announcement in Paris in the summer of 1839, Americans speedily adopted the process of capturing light in dark boxes and fixing images, initially on metal, later on paper. The rest is history, illuminated by Daguerre's art.

The history of Amherst College nearly coincides with that of the photographic medium. It exists on film. It exists because of film, especially so since the advent of Kodaks on campus. Place and history unreel as snapshots framed in the mind.

To say that something happened in "living memory" suggests a sensory picture of it. For many, that memory is essentially visual, primarily photographic. A comment overheard from one proud parent at an Amherst Commencement is typical: "If it wasn't photographed, it didn't happen." Today, more than a century and a half after Daguerre, Commencement, Amherst—indeed our collective past—is unimaginable without the photographic record.

To be sure, there are other sorts of recall. Marcel Proust's evocative lime-blossom tea and madeleine, to wit. For the great French writer, taste persisted when all else failed, "more fragile but more enduring, more unsubstantial, more persistent, more faithful," containing "in the tiny and almost impalpable drop . . . the vast structure of recollection." What are the tasteful remembrances of Amherst past? Pizza, or mystery meat? The Sandwich Man's treats? Burgers from Joe's?

Consider the case of Claude Levi-Strauss's nose. Fifty-plus years after his pioneering work in Brazil, the distinguished anthropologist's notebooks from the field still hint of the creosote with which they were saturated to protect them from termites and mildew. This trace transports Levi-Strauss back to the tropics and to his youth, for the perfume is "the thing itself, still a real part of what I have experienced." How would we make scents of Amherst? Of dusty volumes, or stale beer? In locker room, or painter's studio?

Or, should we trust the ear? Not as auditor of speech which, as any survivor of English 1-2 knows, can be endlessly malleable, maddeningly imprecise, slippery as jelly nailed to a tree. Rather, the ear's response to music: the strains of Haydn or a riff by Coltrane, a Scott Joplin rag or Janis Joplin wail, the driving beat of "Johnny B. Goode." Each might ring true to students of a certain time or place, and as surely as creosote or madeleines transport them backward into a personal past.

But so too might the images of this album, whether the subject is known or not. One may not have performed in Kirby, nor in "Mattie Matix," or Physics I. From the Amherst Common, one might never have marched to war, or against it. Never rowed on the Connecticut, never heard Frost read nor watched the Gym burn, never seined in the sanctuary. Yet in photographs these moments and monuments can be (re)lived and relished. Through photographs, the past survives into the present. Through them, today will be known to tomorrow. Because it was photographed, it did happen, and happens still.

A click of the shutter, and a minstrel forever strums. A dancer flexes, Sabrina passes. Coolidge presides, and Kennedy too. Pelham Hills forever crown the view. Working magic in the darkroom, like an alchemist in the laboratory, the photographer brings these pictures to life. Images emerge slowly in the developing bath, as through the haze of college days, and then are fixed. Chemicals and light and paper are transformed into the stuff of memory.

"What'll I do with just a photograph?" wondered the singer of Irving Berlin's lyric. Today's historians know just what to do, employing the photograph variously to reconstruct the past, or deconstruct it. Archivists are drawn by the image's depictive capacity, considering the photograph as illustration of the past, noting the subject's appearance and its changes over time. The connoisseur studies the print quality and condition, critiques the composition, appraises the photographer's art. Contemporary critics might use it to survey the maker's attitude toward subject. Or to ruminate on the nature of mimetic process. Or to read the images not merely as illustrations of extrinsic events or things, but as cultural texts in their own right.

Take, for instance, two views of residential life, a universal Amherst experience, separated by generations: Delta Upsilon 1880, on page 44, and Ultima Thule 1939, on page 89. The one, a cluttered space; all about, mementoes of travel suggest the trophies of scions new to the global stage. Conspicuous consumption, a Victorian's *horror vacui*, yet oddly vacant. The other, a crowded tableau, heavy with enigmatic mood, worthy of Balthus. Bodies arranged as artfully as bibelots, poses stilled in revery. Decor changes, a Venus yields to Mother, Great Books to comic books. Where The World was once cast aside, the world now intrudes. On the wall, advertisement for trips contemplated but, in 1939, likely deferred, for Europe's *plages incomparables* were soon to be bloodied. Rooms recorded, rooms revealed, yet with their mystery retained.

By their photos, then, we shall know them. The Fairest College as frontier community: students on the border between adolescence and adulthood. A faculty pushing the boundaries of knowledge. An institutional beacon between enlightenment and darkness.

The demands of a book, the tyranny of pagination, necessarily reduce many complexities to binaries. Yin and Yang. Individual and Community. Then and Now. A movie might equally well evoke Amherst, a cinematic unfurling of visual memory. Bound by ties that cannot sever, bound by film and photos. Or collage might suffice, with its disjunctions and overlappings, a bit sloppy perhaps, but more like real life than the pristine page. But in whatever format, it is essentially through vision—the mind's eye, and the photographer's—that we discover and remember Amherst.

Charles C. Eldredge '66
Hall Distinguished Professor of American Art
University of Kansas

1 8 7 3   Varsity rowers practice on the Freshman River.
Crew was popular at Amherst and won many
honors in the 1870s.

1 9 5 0   For more than 30 years, Amherst students enjoyed the
privilege of having Robert Frost in their midst. Here
he reads poetry to a group in the Mead Art Museum's
Rotherwas Room. A television crew filmed the occasion
for the NBC program, "Watch the World."

c. 1 9 5 0 – 5 9   Walker Hall, built between 1868 and 1870, was re-
built after fire gutted the original structure (page 67)
in 1882. Eighty years later the grand old building was
razed to clear the site for the Robert Frost Library.
The idealized 1914 statue of Noah Webster, president of the first Board of Trustees, is still in place.

1 9 7 8   For many years, going back to the middle of the 19th
century, students held bonfire rallies on the eve of athletic
contests. They revived the tradition in 1978, rallying here
at the foot of Memorial Hill the night before the Williams
football game.

c. 1 9 7 8 – 8 3 Nothing dampens the spirit of fans in
the bleachers at Pratt Field.

1917–18   Amherst men prepare for service shortly after the
          nation's entry into World War I. Here the Students'
          Army Training Corps drills in front of the newly
          dedicated Converse Memorial Library.

1 9 7 9   During several days in mid-April, students filled the lobby of Converse Hall to protest campus racism. The protests led to an occupation of the building on April 23 and 24.

1 9 3 7   Geology Professor Frederick Loomis 1896, left, stands
            proudly with the fossil remains of the dinosaur
            Gryposaurus Notabilis in the Pratt Museum of Natural
            History. With Loomis is his faithful assistant, John
            Harlow, who took two years to piece the exhibit together.

1 9 8 1   Elaine Brighty, assistant professor of biology, returns with
students from a field trip to Amherst's wildlife sanctuary.
From the College's earliest days, student naturalists have
explored the surrounding countryside.

1 9 3 2   Three presidents who attended the inauguration of
Stanley King '03, second from left, the College's 11th
chief executive, were two of his predecessors, Alexander
Meiklejohn, far left, and Arthur Stanley Pease. Left out
of King's embrace is Calvin Coolidge 1895, former
President of the United States.

1 9 1 3   Wearing cap-and-gown costumes for their 10th Reunion,
the Class of 1903 parades across Pratt Field before the
Amherst-Dartmouth baseball game.

1 9 1 0   This sparkling reception, "The Lawn Fete," a celebration at the
time of Commencement and Reunions, included graduating
seniors and alumni. Established in 1909, the event was held in
one form or another almost every year until the early 1960s.

1 9 3 8   The great hurricane of September 21 destroyed the
College Grove in the main campus quadrangle. Students
helped with the cleanup after President Stanley King '03
rallied them to "rebuild Amherst College."

1 8 8 8   This track team won the annual New England Intercollegiate Athletic Association games in Worcester, Massachusetts. Frank Delabarre 1890, in the dark shirt, left, broke the record for the two-mile bicycle race. Samuel Warriner 1888, reclining in the foreground, broke records in the pole vault and broad jump.

1 8 9 0   Robert B. Ludington 1891, an outstanding track star,
          sports his costumes as a merry minstrel for a campus show
          that benefited the baseball team. He jokingly described
          himself in an alumni survey, years later, as a "flower . . .
          born to blush unseen."

c. 1 8 8 2   Richard H. Mather 1857, professor of Greek, assembled
one of the country's finest collections of plaster-cast
statues for the study of classical and Renaissance
sculpture. It was displayed for many years in this gallery
on the top floor of Williston Hall.

1 9 0 3   Student Tom Brown '04 took this picture of his geology

professor, B. K. Emerson 1865, on a field trip. By the

time Emerson retired in 1917, he had taught at Amherst

for 47 years.

c. 1 8 8 5 — 8 7   Freshmen equipped with T-squares and drawing boards study geometry in Williston Hall under the tutelage of their young instructor, James H. Tufts 1884.

1 9 5 1   "Go Purple! Go White!" Cheerleader Milton Moss '53
        exhorts the Amherst crowd at a home football game.

1 9 2 1   Jeffery John Archer Amherst, styled Viscount Holmesdale,
later the fifth Earl Amherst, acknowledges the Amherst
Centennial crowd at the baseball game against Wesleyan.
A descendant of the original Lord Jeff, and guest of honor
for the Centennial, he agreed to throw out the first ball.

1 8 7 4 – 7 5   Homer C. Strong, left, and Frank A. Hosmer pose
for the Class of 1875 album. When they became
sophomores, members of each class distinguished
themselves as upperclassmen by sporting distinctive
class hats and canes.

1 9 2 5 – 2 6   The Class of 1920 chose a nautical theme and costume for its Reunion. Here Roland Wood, Charles Reed, and Kenneth Low model the uniforms for a newsletter that said these three-dollar outfits could be ordered in time for the Reunion.

c. 1 8 7 8   The interior of Stearns Church, which was dedicated in
1873, was the scene of College worship services until the
church was torn down in 1948 to make way for the Mead
Art Building. The steeple, with chimes given in memory
of Amherst men who died in the Civil War, remains
standing.

c. 1 8 5 7   The early missionaries to eastern Turkey posing stiffly
here include four Amherst graduates: Elias Riggs 1829,
first row, second from left; Henry Van Lennep 1837, first
row, far right; Isaac Bliss 1844, second row, second from
left; and his brother Edwin Bliss 1837, second row,
second from right.

c. 1 9 7 8 – 8 3 Though this open-air event is not identified, it
probably was similar to "The New Games" at
Memorial Field—activities organized for freshman orientation during the middle to late 1980s.

1 9 7 0   This rally on the Amherst Town Common was part of the
nationwide student antiwar protest prompted by the U. S.
bombing of Cambodia and student deaths at Kent State
University.

c. 1 8 6 6   A student wag put the heads of two faculty members,
the brothers L. Clark Seelye, left, and Julius Seelye 1849,
on Raphael's cherubs. Clark, a professor of rhetoric and
English, became the first president of Smith College in
1875. A year later, Julius, who taught philosophy and
metaphysics, became the fifth president of Amherst.

1 9 4 0   On the front lawn of their fraternity, members of Phi
Kappa Psi spoof team portraits of the 19th century.

c. 1 9 0 0 — 1 0   Edward "Doc" Hitchcock 1849, best remembered as the College's pioneering professor of hygiene and physical education, was also an avid musician. A tribute in the *Amherst Graduate's Quarterly* said no one was "more instrumental . . . in founding and promoting the Department of Music" than beloved "Old Doc." Colleagues remembered that "he used to gather his family and students and members of the Faculty in his home, and lead them in Sunday evening music, vocal and instrumental."

c. 1 8 7 5   Professors lived along this part of Route 9, or College
Street, in the late 19th century, so it was known as
"Faculty Street." Grosvenor House, in the foreground,
remains, but Valentine Hall and Moore Dormitory now
stand where the other houses were.

c. 1 8 8 0   In the 1880s *The Amherst Student* complained of noise
in the Reading Room of the Morgan Library and admon-
ished students: "Do your talking elsewhere, but be silent
here." Morgan was built in 1853 at a cost of $10,000.

1 9 1 2   At its 10th Reunion, the Class of 1902 sported these
uniforms called "yama yama" costumes. A spirited
bunch, the class won the Reunion Trophy for the
strongest turnout: 81 percent. This class originated
the idea of wearing Reunion outfits in 1905.

1 8 8 9   Amherst students hired and decorated this train to take
them to Springfield, Massachusetts, for the Harvard-Yale
football game. The faculty rescheduled Saturday classes
so that all could make the trip. Yale won the contest, 6-0.

c. 1 8 8 5 – 8 9 Amherst was the first institution to have a physical
education program for college students. It was
developed by Edward "Doc" Hitchcock 1849,
right foreground, who drilled classes in the new
Pratt Gymnasium.

1 9 8 6   LeFred Wilson Jr. '87 and others rehearse a dance,
"Structuring," that they choreographed for the annual
spring Student-Faculty Dance Concert in Kirby Theater.

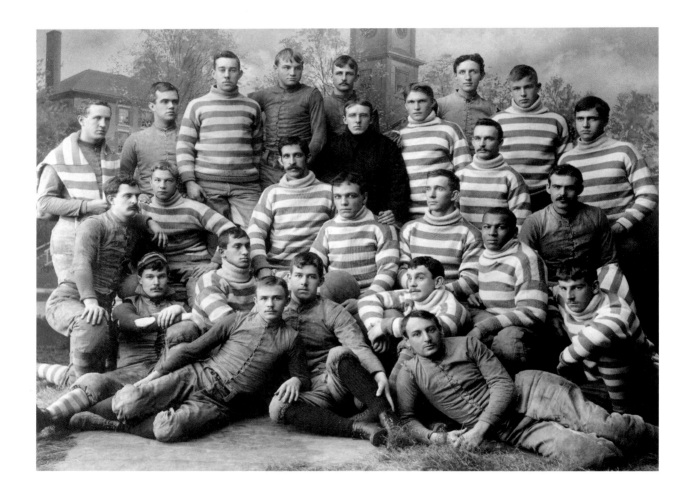

1 8 9 1   Captain William H. Lewis 1892, with ball, center, led this
Amherst football team to a tie against Williams in 1891.
The team demolished the Ephmen, 60-0, the following
year. Lewis went on to become the country's first African-
American Assistant Attorney General.

Broad Jump 23 Ft. 2½ in. NEI Record 1905
W. P. Hubbard.

1905   Walter Hubbard '06 sets the broad jump record, 23' 2 ½",
at the New England intercollegiate track meet in Worcester,
Massachusetts. A large contingent of students attended
the events and, "Time and again," *The Amherst Student*
reported, "the long Amherst yell swept over the course."

1 9 7 6   The College became coeducational in 1975. Thanks to
the order of the alphabet, Anita Cilderman '76, a transfer
student from Mount Holyoke College, was the first
woman to receive a bachelor's diploma from Amherst.
Here she celebrates the historic moment with President
John William Ward.

1 9 1 2   Undergraduates wear their Sunday best to march at the
          inauguration of Alexander Meiklejohn, eighth president
          of the College. The procession of dignitaries, faculty and
          students extended from College Row to College Hall.

1 9 5 8 – 5 9   Douglas Williams '56 stands with Japanese students
from Amherst House at Doshisha University. After World
War II, he was the first alumnus to resume the tradition of
Amherst Fellows at the Doshisha.

1 8 8 o   This is believed to be the room of a senior, James Turner
            1880, in the Delta Upsilon fraternity. The Victorian
            clutter includes the student's top hat, a standard item in
            an upperclassman's wardrobe.

1 8 6 8 – 7 2   Charles E. Garman 1872, flanked here by unidentified classmates, became a celebrated Amherst professor of moral philosophy. An obituary in 1907 praised "his rare ability in developing in others the desire and the power of thinking for themselves."

1 9 2 1   This Amherst swimming team was undefeated for the
            second straight season and tied for second place in the
            National Intercollegiate Championships.

1 9 6 6   Richard Ball '68 pitches against a University of Massachusetts team that defeated Amherst, 2-0. The College's
baseball tradition goes back to 1859 when Amherst
defeated Williams, 73-32, in America's first intercollegiate baseball game—a three-hour contest held in
Pittsfield, Massachusetts.

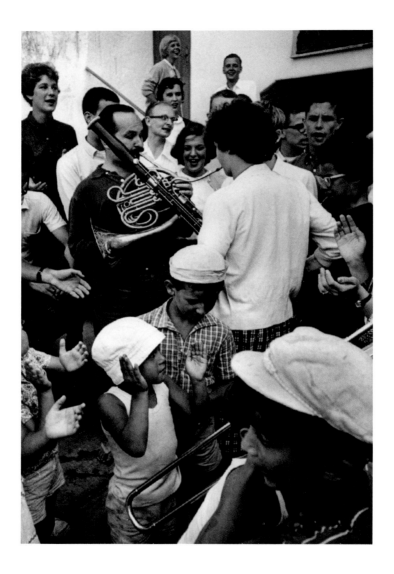

1 9 6 1   In a spontaneous street concert, the Amherst-Smith

Chamber Singers entertain young villagers upon arriving in

Capri, where they performed at the Spoleto Festival. The

July visit was part of the Singers' European tour that

summer.

1 9 8 7   Dickens Mathieu '87 speaks at the April dedication of the
College's African-American cultural residence, Charles
Drew House, formerly Phi Alpha Psi. Dr. Drew '26 was
 a medical scientist whose pioneering work made possible
the preservation of blood plasma.

1 8 8 5   In this student production of Sheridan's comedy, "The
Rivals," W. Clyde Fitch 1886, left, the future playwright,
had the role of Lydia Languish. An *Amherst Student*
reviewer wrote that the female characters were "the most
creditable attainments" of the production.

c. 1 8 5 0   The gaze of this unidentified student, a member of
the Class of 1850, is still penetrating after nearly 150
years. Daguerreotype portraits were made of all 25
members of the class, and all of them are held in the
College Archives.

c. 1 8 7 3   For most of the 19th century, the College Well,
immediately east of Johnson Chapel, was a popular
landmark. Students stopped here to drink its
refreshment and to read or post notices.

1 8 9 2   This track and field team boasted many champions. One
was cyclist George D. Pratt 1893, upper right, who set a
New England record for the two-mile bicycle race. At
the far left is their trainer, Dwight Newport.

1 9 8 3   To develop class unity among the freshmen, deans teach them "the lap game" at Memorial Field during Orientation. The idea was that if they formed a tight circle and "sat down" simultaneously, they would all support each other.

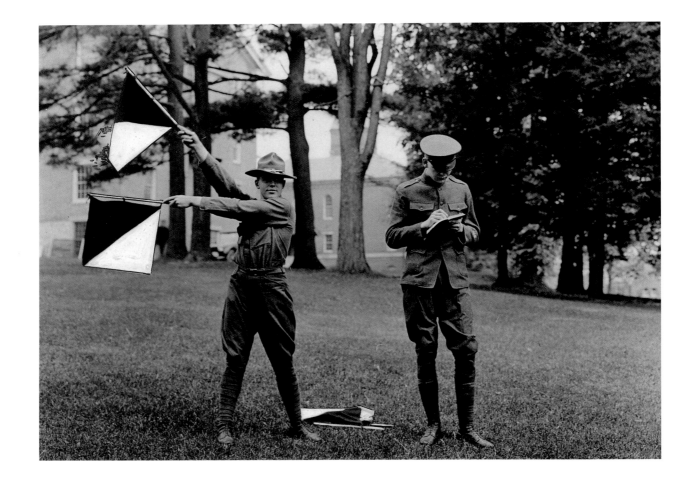

1 9 1 7 — 1 8   During World War I, the College introduced students
to military training by adding special courses, including
signal practice, to the curriculum.

1 9 7 9   Whisked onto campus by three members of the "even" Class of 1980, this Sabrina statue made a flying stop to taunt the "odd" Class of 1979 at its Commencement. But six days later another Sabrina—the real McCoy?—showed up for Reunion Weekend.

c. 1 8 6 6   This cartoon montage of an Amherst College Faculty

Meeting, one of several humorous works by a student,

Charles H. Allen 1869, shows a boxers' handshake between

Edward "Doc" Hitchcock 1849, professor of hygiene and

physical education, right, and an undergraduate, Daniel

Smart 1867.

C. 1 9 6 0 – 6 2   A member of the Class of 1964 stresses a point
during a lecture class in Fayerweather Hall. These
"core curriculum" classes also met separately in
smaller seminars.

1 8 8 1 – 8 2   "Velocipede mania" hit Amherst in 1868. By 1882 there was
an organized bicycle club at the College. *The Amherst Student* said
the beginning cyclist "knows he must bite the dust and come out
maimed . . . but others have been through it and conquered."

1 9 6 9   This year's Amherst rugby players (in narrow stripes)
enjoyed a successful 8-4-1 season. The popular club sport
was introduced at the College in 1956.

1 9 4 5   Forty cargo vessels that were built for service in World
War II were named for American colleges. The new,
10,500-ton *Amherst Victory* was launched from a shipyard
at Terminal Island, California, on February 28. Amherst
provided the crew with a shipboard library.

1 9 1 5   In the quadrangle outside Walker Hall, Harold A.
         Lyon '15 delivers the Grove Oration at the seniors' Class
         Day exercises. The tradition of seniors choosing one of
         their classmates to deliver a humorous address on Class
         Day dates back to the early 1860s.

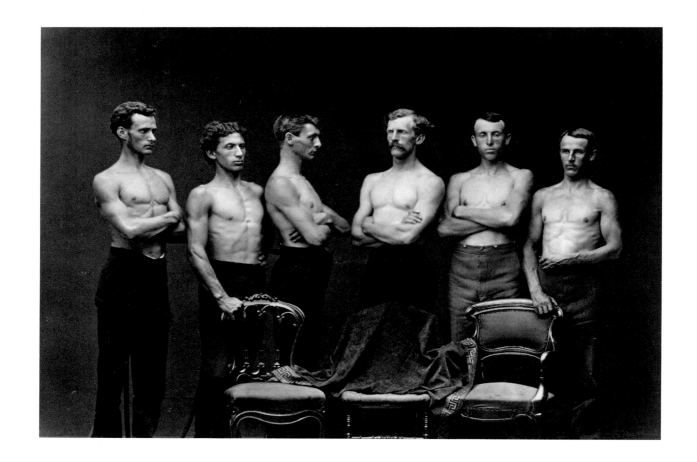

1 8 7 2   This championship crew trounced Harvard, Yale, and
all other contestants at the 1872 regatta in Springfield,
Massachusetts. One report said analysts "attributed
Amherst's superiority to the constant exercise of its
undergraduates in the Gymnasium."

c. 1 8 8 7 – 8 9   Amherst athletes Royal Watkins 1889, left, and Everett White 1889 starred in football, track, baseball, and "heavy gym." Interestingly, neither belonged to the Tennis Association.

c. 1 8 8 o   Walker Hall, the College's "Temple of Science," was built between 1868 and 1870 at an extravagant cost of $125,000 ("almost more than the rest of the college buildings combined," marveled historian William S. Tyler). The building was supposed to be indestructible, but it succumbed to a disastrous fire in 1882 and had to be rebuilt. The second Walker Hall appears on page 3.

C. 1 9 0 4   Alumni who had souvenirs of their athletic triumphs
helped a College committee furnish this Trophy Room in
Pratt Gymnasium. *The Amherst Student* reported that the
committee "just missed getting the first football ever
played with at Amherst." The committee members wrote
to the alumnus who had the ball, but his wife had burned
the trophy only hours before he received the letter.

1 9 9 4   Jennifer Almiron '98 moves the ball in soccer against the
Mount Holyoke Lyons. Amherst's 10-0 victory was
one of many leading the Lady Jeffs to the Little Three
Championship and the "Sweet Sixteen" of an NCAA
Division III tournament.

c. 1 8 7 7 – 7 8   Members of Alpha Delta Phi lived in this house from
1875 until fire destroyed it in 1924. It was reputed to be
the earliest residential fraternity building in the country.
The brothers here include the future benefactor of the
Folger Shakespeare Library, Henry Clay Folger 1879,
sitting on the rail fence.

1943–44   During World War II the living room of Theta Delta Chi
served as a barracks for Companies A and B of the Army's
Area and Language Studies Unit.

c. 1 8 7 9   Much as it is today, "Merchants Row" along Broadway
(now South Pleasant Street) in downtown Amherst was a
center for banking and shopping by both townspeople
and students.

1 9 2 8   The administrative team that directed College business in the 1920s enjoys Christmas tea at the President's House. From the left are: Thomas C. Esty 1893, dean of the College; Edith Churchill, secretary to William J. Newlin 1899, the director of admission; Gladys Kimball, recorder; President George D. Olds; Ruth Butterworth, the president's secretary; and Newlin. Olds, Esty and Newlin were all mathematics professors.

1 9 8 7   Students plan strategy for the three-legged race in the
"Clash of the Classes." Initiated in 1982, the games
renewed a College tradition of rivalry between freshmen
and sophomores.

c. 1 8 8 4   Clay Hollister 1886 examines a rock specimen on a
geology field trip in the Pelham Hills near Amherst.

1 8 8 3   Sophomores traditionally celebrated the conclusion of
their compulsory mathematics course by "mourning" its
end. In 1883 the costumed ceremony, "In Memoriam De
Mattie Matix," was directed by the recumbent W. Clyde
Fitch 1886, center. This event included the cremation of
a "corpse" and a midnight funeral procession of horse-
drawn floats led by the town band.

1 9 3 8   When *The Amherst Student* alerted the administration
to severe overcrowding in the reading room of Converse
Memorial Library, President Stanley King '03 solved the
problem by establishing this reading room for freshmen
in the former Mather Art Gallery, on the top floor of
Williston Hall.

c. 1 8 6 9   This southwesterly view of the campus buildings shows
the rustic nature of the College's early surroundings.
From the left along the summit are the Octagon,
Williston Hall, Chapel Row, and Appleton Cabinet.

1 9 6 3   Poet Archibald MacLeish and President John F. Kennedy
share a light moment at a special College convocation on
October 26. Later that day they celebrated a ground-
breaking ceremony for the Robert Frost Library. Kennedy
said he hoped that the students "who come into this
library will touch something of distinction in our national
life, and, I hope, give something to it."

1 9 6 3   A silent vigil of about sixty students and faculty members
waits for President Kennedy to arrive at Amherst. They
demonstrated to show their support for the President and
his civil rights bill.

c. 1 8 6 9 – 7 3   Appleton Cabinet housed the College's Hitchcock
Ichnological Cabinet of fossil footprints, the Gilbert
Museum of Indian Relics, and the Adams Zoological
Museum. Many of the animals on display were collected
by alumni serving as missionaries around the globe.

1 9 4 9   The Amherst College Masquers perform at the Folger
Shakespeare Theater in a landmark, NBC-televised
production of "Julius Caesar." It was the first production
ever staged in the theater, and the first Shakespeare play
ever performed in its entirety for television.

c. 1 9 0 6 — 0 7   When it opened in 1906, the "natatorium" in the base-
ment of Pratt Gymnasium was one of the best college
swimming pools in the country. The walls were painted
yellow and terra cotta to resemble the ancient baths of
Rome.

c. 1 8 7 9   Behind Johnson Chapel, a photographer took this view
looking through the College Grove toward East College.
Patches in the lawn were probably worn bare by generations of students playing games.

1 9 8 1   In the stillness of winter, students walk to Pratt Pool
and the New Gymnasium.

1 9 8 5   A spectacular pre-dawn fire destroyed the New Gymnasium on March 9. LeFrak Gymnasium replaced the
building two years later. The fire also damaged Pratt
Pool, but firefighters from six communities managed to
save the rest of the athletic complex.

1 8 9 8   Concerts given by the Mandolin Club may have

inspired the Amherst song, "First Memory."

    Aye! college life is mirrored brightly
    In college songs, with frolic rife;
    One sweet guitar will tell you rightly
    The secret charm of college life.

1 9 3 9   In early days this room was known as "Ultima Thule"—
the College's farthermost place. It is 30 South College,
at the top southwest corner of the first campus building.
Here the first senior recitations were held, societies met,
and fraternities were founded.

1 8 9 6   These Amherst students joined hundreds of other
collegians for the Northfield Students' Conference
in East Northfield, Massachusetts. The encamp-
ment was an annual meeting for Bible study and
recreation. According to *The Amherst Student*, "living
in the open air was especially enjoyed by our men,
who stood well to the front in the intercollegiate
athletic contests."

c. 1 9 3 9   When completed in 1905, the College Observatory
housed New England's largest telescope. It had a focal
length of 24 feet and an 18-inch glass. Astronomy
Professor David Todd 1875 designed and equipped the
building and raised most of the funds for the project.

1 9 4 7 "Memorial Field is dedicated by the Alumni to the
Amherst men who in two great wars gallantly responded
to their country's call."

— Inscription at the War Memorial overlooking
Memorial Field and the Holyoke Range

94

c. 1 8 8 5   In the late 1800s, class delegations in the fraternities
wrote and staged plays and pantomimes every winter.
This scene is from the Alpha Delta Phi play, "Always
Take Mother's Advice," performed by brothers from
the Class of 1888.

1 9 2 5   Freshman-sophomore rivalries took the form of "flag rush" in the early 1900s. A pennant painted with the sophomore class year was tied to a nine-foot pole set up at Pratt Field, where the freshmen tried to take it by force. Years later an alumnus remembered how the sophomores "twined arms around the post and stood tense and nervous for the attack."

1 9 6 6   The legendary "Darp"—James E. Ostendarp, head
football coach—compiled a record of 168-91-5 in his
33 years at Amherst. He never let Amherst games be
televised because "We're in education," he said, "we
aren't in the entertainment business."

1 9 9 0   Toby Unger '93, the first woman to be the College's Lord
Jeff mascot, cheers the football team against Bates in the
opening game of the season. John Whitney '82 created
the mascot's role in 1980.

1 8 8 8   Robert B. Ludington 1891 took this picture of Spring
Street after the Blizzard of 1888, which dumped 38
inches of snow on Amherst. Accounts say that for the
first time in history, the College cancelled chapel and
closed for the day.

1 8 9 2   College Librarian William I. Fletcher sits in front of
Morgan Library, surrounded by his students in the
Amherst Summer School Department of Library
Economy. The school, established by Fletcher, offered
professional training for librarians from 1891 to 1905.

1 8 8 8   The Spartan rooms of early Amherst eventually gave way
            to fancier quarters. Here, at Mrs. G. C. Munsell's
            rooming house, Charles L. Bliss 1888 enjoyed a home
            away from home.

c. 1 8 8 5 – 8 8 Country rides were a favorite student pastime. These Chi Phi brothers may be planning a scenic trip to Mount Holyoke or Mount Tom. The group includes W. P. Bigelow 1889, far left, who became an Amherst professor of music, and his classmate George B. Churchill, far right, later a professor of English.

1 8 8 4   These students, all members of the Class of 1886, display
cats they have dissected for their junior biology class,
taught by Professor John M. Tyler 1873. They must have
learned their lessons well. Five of the seven later became
surgeons; another taught biology and zoology at Smith
College for thirty years.

103

1 9 8 4   Behind Fayerweather Hall, students model headdresses they
made for a sculpture class taught by Assistant Professor
James W. Sullivan, left. The Fine Arts Department was
established in 1929 and offered its first studio art class
six years later.

C. 1 8 7 7   This view to the northwest from Johnson Chapel is
little changed to this day. It includes the Octagon, the
President's House, the College (later Morgan) Library,
and College Hall.

1 9 1 0   When senior caps and gowns were first introduced at
Amherst in 1892, the *Amherst Literary Monthly* praised the
innovation, saying the academic costume "gives a certain
dignity to the wearer, and makes the sight of a gathering of
Seniors an impressive one." Seniors were less reverent,
however. By 1910 they had established this Commencement tradition called the "Gambol on the Green."

All photographs are from the Amherst College Archives, which has assigned their titles. Dimensions are in inches; height precedes width.

Cover and Frontispiece, College Hill from the Northwest, c. 1878; J. L. Lovell, Photographers; albumen print, 5 ¼ x 7 ⅝

p. 1, Varsity Rowers, 1873; J. L. Lovell, Photographers; albumen print, 5 ¾ x 7 ¾

p. 2, Robert Frost, 1950; Frost Photographic Service; gelatin silver print, 7 ½ x 9 ½

p. 3, Second Walker Hall, c. 1950–59; Edward Thayer Monroe; gelatin silver print, 10 ¼ x 13 ¼

p. 4, Bonfire, November 10, 1978; Delia Baroni; gelatin silver print; 5 ⅞ x 8 ⅞

p. 5, Students in the Rain, c. 1978–83; Gabriel Cooney; gelatin silver print, 5 ½ x 8

p. 6, Converse Drill, 1917–18; Gordon Photographers; gelatin silver contact print, 3 ¾ x 4 ¾

p. 7, Converse Occupation, April 23, 1979; photographer unknown; gelatin silver print, 9 x 6

p. 8, Dinosaur, June 2, 1937; Lincoln W. Barnes; gelatin silver contact print, 5 x 7

p. 9, Biology Field Trip, 1981; Gabriel Cooney; gelatin silver print, 6 ¾ x 8 ¾

p. 10, King Inauguration Notables, November 11, 1932; Wide World Photos; gelatin silver print, 6 x 8

p. 11, Class of 1903 Decennial Reunion, June 21, 1913; Homer Smith '15; gelatin silver print, 2 ¾ x 4 ⅜

p. 12, The Lawn Fete, June 28, 1910; photographer unknown; gelatin silver print, 4 ½ x 6 ½

p. 13, Hurricane Damage, September 22, 1938; Lincoln W. Barnes; gelatin silver contact print, 7 x 5

p. 15, 1888 Athletic (Track) Team, 1888; Notman Photographic Co.; albumen print, 7 ½ x 9 ½

p. 16, left, Robert B. Ludington 1891, in Dress, 1890; photographer unknown; albumen print, 7 ½ x 4 ⅜

p. 16, right, Robert B. Ludington 1891, with Banjo, 1890; photographer unknown; albumen print, 7 ½ x 4 ⅜

p. 17, Mather Art Gallery, c. 1882; J. L. Lovell, Photographers; albumen print, 9 x 7

p. 18, B. K. Emerson 1865 in the Field, 1903, (reprinted for card, 1910); Thomas C. Brown '04; gelatin silver print photo postcard, 2 ½ x 2 ½

p. 19, J. H. Tufts 1884 Instructs His Mathematics Class, c. 1885–87; J. L. Lovell, Photographers; albumen print, 7 ¼ x 9 ½

p. 20, Cheerleader Milton Oscar Moss '53, 1951; photographer unknown; gelatin silver print, 9 ½ x 7 ⅝

p. 21, Viscount Holmesdale, June 21, 1921; Gordon Photographers; gelatin silver print, 3 ¾ x 4 ⅞

p. 22, Hats and Canes, 1874–75; J. L. Lovell, Photographers; albumen print, 7 ½ x 5 ¾

p. 23, Class of 1920 Shipmates, 1925–26; photographer unknown; gelatin silver print, 6 ⅝ x 4 ⅛

p. 24, College (Stearns) Church Interior, c. 1878; J. L. Lovell, Photographers; albumen print, 4 x 7 ⅛

p. 25, Missionaries, c. 1857; Abdullah Freres; salt print, 9 ⅞ x 13, oval

p. 26, Dancing in a Line, c. 1978–83; Gabriel Cooney; gelatin silver print, 5 ¾ x 8 ⅝

p. 27, Rally on the Common, May 6, 1970; Blaine K. Rawdon '73; gelatin silver print, 6 ¼ x 9 ⅛

p. 28, Seelye Brothers Caricature by an Unknown Artist, c. 1866; J. L. Lovell, Photographers; albumen print from composite sketch and photographic prints, 2 ¼ x 3 ⅝

p. 29, Football Parody, November 3, 1940; Lincoln W. Barnes; gelatin silver print, 7 x 9

p. 31, Professor Edward "Doc" Hitchcock 1849, c. 1900–10; Mary Allen; platinum print, 8 x 5 ⅞

p. 32, Faculty Street, c. 1875; J. L. Lovell, Photographers; albumen print, 5 ¼ x 7 ¾

p. 33, College (Morgan) Library Stacks, c. 1880; Notman Photographic Co.; albumen print, 7 ¼ x 9 ½

p. 34, "Yama Yama" Costumes, June 24, 1912; photographer unknown; toned gelatin silver print, 9 x 11 ½

p. 35, 'A' Train to Harvard-Yale Game, November 23, 1889; photographer unknown; cyanotype, 5 x 8

p. 36, Hygiene and Physical Education Class, c. 1885–89; Notman Photographic Co.; albumen print, 7 ½ x 9 ½

p. 37, LeFred Wilson Jr. '87 Dancing, 1986; Frank Ward; gelatin silver print, 5 ¾ x 8 ½

p. 38, 1891 Football Team, 1891; G. Waldon Smith, Photographers; albumen print, 9 ½ x 13

p. 39, W. P. Hubbard '06 Broad Jumping, May 20, 1905; photographer unknown; toned matte collodion print, 7 ½ x 9 ⅝

p. 41, First Woman Graduate, Anita Cilderman '76, June 6, 1976; Robert E. Kingman '72; silver gelatin print, 6 x 9

p. 42, Meiklejohn Inauguration Procession, October 16, 1912; photographer unknown; gelatin silver print, 3 ¾ x 11 ⅜

p. 43, Douglas Williams '56 at Doshisha, 1958–59; [Roland H. Barrett]; gelatin silver print, 5 ¾ x 8 ¾

p. 44, Student Room with Top Hat, 1880; Notman Photographic Co.; albumen print, 4 ½ x 7 ⅜

p. 45, Charles Garman 1872 as a Student, 1868–72; Ramsdell's Ferrotype and Photograph Gallery; tintype, 3 ½ x 2 ½

p. 46, 1921 Swim Team, 1921; Webster's Studios; toned gelatin silver print, 7 ½ x 9 ⅜

p. 47, Baseball Action, April 12, 1966; James Gerhard '64; gelatin silver print, 7 ½ x 8 ½

p. 48, Glee Club in Capri, July 12, 1961; Carlo Bavagnoli for *LIFE*; gelatin silver print, 13 ¼ x 8 ⅞

p. 49, Charles Drew House Dedication, April 18, 1987; Eric Krody '84; gelatin silver print, 6 ¼ x 9 ½

p. 50, "The Rivals," 1885; W. H. Baker, Photographers; albumen print, 7 ¼ x 9 ⅜

p. 51, Unidentified Member of the Class of 1850, c. 1850; photographer unknown; daguerreotype, 2 ¾ x 2 ¼

p. 53, College Well, c. 1873; J. L. Lovell, Photographers; albumen print, 7 ¾ x 5 ¾

p. 54, 1892 Athletic (Track) Team, 1892; G. Waldon Smith, Photographers; albumen print, 9 ½ x 13

p. 55, The Lap Game, September 6, 1983; Gabriel Cooney; gelatin silver print, 5 ½ x 8 ⅛

p. 56, World War I Signal Training, c. 1917–18; photographer unknown; gelatin silver print (retouched), 4 ¾ x 6 ⅝

p. 57, Sabrina and the Helicopter, May 27, 1979; Delia Baroni; gelatin silver print, 6 ½ x 9

p. 58, Amherst College Faculty Meeting Caricature by Charles H. Allen 1869, c. 1866; J. L. Lovell, Photographers; albumen print from composite sketch and photographic prints, 5 ½ x 6 ½

p. 59, A Student with a Question, c. 1960–62; Hanson Carroll; gelatin silver print, 13 ⅜ x 19 ½

p. 60, Bicycle Club, 1881–82; G. W. Pach and Brothers, Photographers; albumen print, 6 ¾ x 9

p. 61, Rugby Club, 1969; [James Gerhard '64]; gelatin silver print, 7 ½ x 9 ⅜

p. 62, USS Amherst Victory, February 28, 1945; photographer unknown; gelatin silver print, 9 ⅝ x 6 ⅞

p. 63, Grove Oration, June 29, 1915; photographer unknown; gelatin silver print, 7 ⅝ x 9 ⅝

p. 64, Rowing Champions, Studio View, 1872; J. L. Lovell, Photographers; albumen print, 5 ¾ x 7 ¾

p. 65, Tennis Players, c. 1887–89; G. H. Baker, Photographer; tintype, 3 ½ x 2 ½

p. 67, First Walker Hall, c. 1880; G. W. Pach and Brothers, Photographers; albumen print, 7 x 9

p. 68, Athletic Trophy Room, c. 1904; photographer unknown; toned gelatin silver print, 7 ½ x 9 ½

p. 69, Soccer Action, Jennifer (Jen) Almiron '98, October 13, 1994; Geoffrey Bluh; gelatin silver print, 6 ¼ x 9 ½

p. 70, Sellen House, Alpha Delta Phi, c. 1877–78; J. L. Lovell, Photographers; albumen print, 8 x 5 ⅜

p. 71, World War II Quarters, 1943–44; Edwin C. Van Valey '47; gelatin silver contact print, 5 x 7

p. 72, 19th Century Downtown Amherst, c. 1879; G. W. Pach and Brothers, Photographers; albumen print, 5 ¼ x 8 ¼

p. 73, President's Christmas Tea, 1928; Kinsman Studios; toned gelatin silver print, 7 ⅜ x 9 ⅜

p. 74, Clash of the Classes, May 3, 1987; Frank Ward; gelatin silver print, 8 ⅞ x 6

p. 75, Geology Student in the Field, c. 1884; photographer unknown; albumen print, 4 ⅜ x 7 ⅜

p. 77, The Burial of Mattie Matix, 1883; photographer unknown; albumen print, 7 x 9 ⅛

p. 78, Freshman Reading Room, 1938; Lincoln W. Barnes; gelatin silver contact print, 4 ¾ x 6 ½

p. 79, College Row from the Southwest, c. 1869; J. L. Lovell, Photographers; albumen print, 5 ½ x 7 ⅝

p. 80, Archibald MacLeish and President Kennedy, October 26, 1963; [Patrick DeLeon '64]; gelatin silver print, 7 ⅝ x 9 ½

p. 81, Civil Rights Demonstration, October 26, 1963; [*Amherst Student* staff]; gelatin silver print, 6 ⅞ x 9 ½

p. 82, Appleton Cabinet Interior, c. 1869–73; J. L. Lovell, Photographers; albumen print, 5 ¾ x 7 ¾

p. 83, Masquers' Television Production of "Julius Caesar," 1949; Reni Newsphoto Services; gelatin silver print, 9 x 7 ⅛

p. 84, Swimmers at First Pratt Pool, c. 1906–07; photographer unknown; gelatin silver print, 4 ⅞ x 8 ¾

p. 85, The Grove, c. 1879; J. L. Lovell, Photographers; albumen print, 5 ⅜ x 8

p. 86, Gymnasium Complex in the Snow, 1981; Gabriel Cooney; gelatin silver print, 6 x 9

p. 87, New Gymnasium Fire, March 9, 1985; Frank Ward; gelatin silver print, 6 ⅛ x 9 ¼

p. 88, Mandolin Club, 1898; J. L. Lovell, Photographers; albumen print, 9 ¾ x 13

p. 89, Ultima Thule (30 South College), 1939; James H. Feasley '41; gelatin silver print, 7 ½ x 9 ⅜

p. 91, Camp Northfield, 1896; Arthur W. Yale; albumen print, 4 ½ x 6 ½

p. 92, Observatory Telescope, c. 1939; W. E. Corbin; toned gelatin silver print, 10 x 8

p. 93, War Memorial and Holyoke Range, 1947; Edward Thayer Monroe; gelatin silver print, 7 ⅝ x 9 ⅜

p. 94, "Always Take Mother's Advice," c. 1885; J. L. Lovell, Photographers; albumen print, 3 ½ x 4 ⅜

p. 95, Flag Rush, September 26, 1925; Lincoln W. Barnes; toned gelatin silver print, 5 x 7

p. 96, Coach Ostendarp, October 29, 1966; Jim Gerhard '64; gelatin silver print, 6 ⅛ x 9 ¼

p. 97, Toby Unger '93 as Lord Jeffery Amherst, September 22, 1990; Beth Grace; gelatin silver print, 6 ½ x 9 ½

p. 98, Aftermath of the Great Blizzard, March 14, 1888; Robert B. Ludington 1891; albumen print, 4 ⅞ x 7 ¼

p. 99, Fletcher Library School, 1892; photographer unknown; albumen print, 6 ¼ x 9

p. 100, No Fishing Allowed, 1888; G. W. Pach and Brothers, Photographers; albumen print, 7 ⅝ x 9 ⅛

p. 101, Group Excursion, c. 1885–88; photographer unknown; albumen print, 6 ⅞ x 9 ⅜

p. 102, Biology Class, 1884; photographer unknown; albumen print, 3 ¾ x 4 ¾

p. 103, Art Class, 1984; Frank Ward; gelatin silver print, 7 ¼ x 7 ¼

p. 104, View from Chapel Looking Northwest, c. 1877; J. L. Lovell, Photographers; albumen print, 5 ½ x 8

p. 105, Gambol on the Green, 1910; Justin B. Smith '09; gelatin silver print, 4 ¼ x 6 ¼

THE 175TH ANNIVERSARY BOOK COMMITTEE

Suzanne Auerbach

Daria D'Arienzo

Emily de Rotstein

Anne Monahan

Kristin V. Rehder

Douglas C. Wilson '62

Research

Peter Weis

Designed by

Triebert Ross Design

Typeset in Monotype Centaur

Printed on Quintessence, a paper that meets the requirements
of ANSI/NISO Z39.48–1992
*American National Standard for Permanence of Paper for Publications
and Documents in Libraries and Archives.*

∞